· Shelf Life ·

Concept by Rosie Walford,
Paula Benson and Paul West.
Text by Rosie Walford.
Art direction by Paul West and
Paula Benson at Form®.
Design by Claire Warner, Paul West
and Paula Benson at Form®.
Photography by Alan Bray at AB Digital.
First published in Great Britain 2004.
© 2004 by Shelf Life Collective Limited.

Bloomsbury Publishing Plc,
38 Soho Square, London W1D 3HB.

ISBN 0 7475 7516 9
10 9 8 7 6 5 4 3 2 1

Printed by C&C Offset Printing
Company Ltd, China.

All papers used by Bloomsbury
Publishing are natural, recyclable
products made from wood grown
in well-managed forests. The
manufacturing processes conform
to the environmental regulations
of the country of origin.

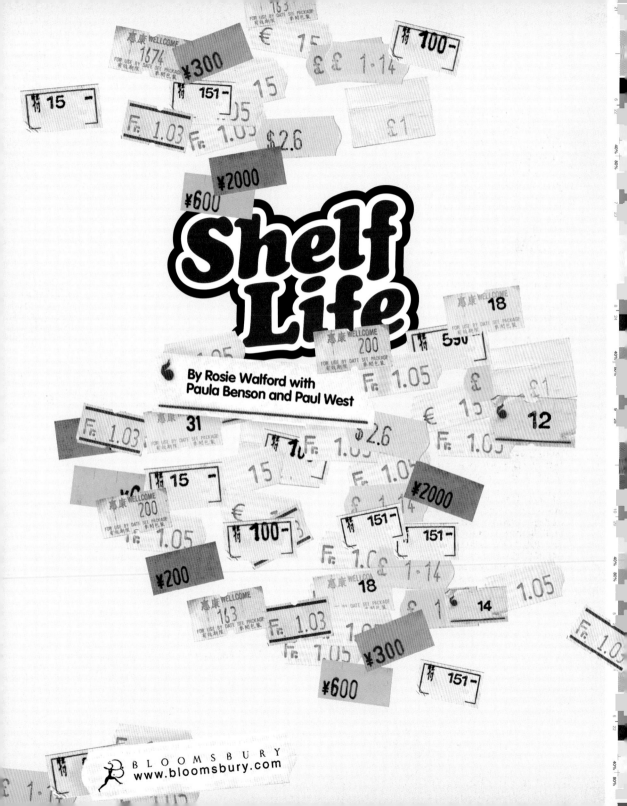

Shelf Life

By Rosie Walford with
Paula Benson and Paul West

BLOOMSBURY
www.bloomsbury.com

This book is dedicated to all the independent businesses which keep the world a diverse and entertaining place.

Cover

Contents

Introduction to an Endangered Species — P 6

113 Heroes of the Supermarket World — P 10

Population Density –
Where Shelf Life was found — 138

From Shop Shelf to Bookshelf — P 1.40

Acknowledgements — P 1.41

Index — P 1.42

About the Collectors — P 1.44

▼Page 06   ▼Page 10   ▼Page 138

▼Page 140   ▼Page 142

Featuring
113
packets from
a much wider
collection

xxxxxxxxxxxx   xxxxx

xxxxxxxxxxxx   xxxxxx   xxxxx

MANUFACTURER'S PROMISE
The products in this book are genuine hand-picked goods,
photographed fresh from the rucksacks in which they
travelled. We have used no artificial smoke, mirrors
or retouching.

xxxxxxxxxxxxxxxxxxxxx   xxxxxxxxxxxx

Introduction to Shelf Life -
An Endangered Species

What was the Peruvian brand manager referring to when he named his delicious tuna Grated Fanny? Do Italians cleaning their bathrooms with Smac or Toke scrub with wilder eyes? Would you market your new soap powder as Barf, your flavoursome chocolate as Chubi or Plopp?

These packets, tins, boxes and bottles are ordinary household groceries loved by shoppers from Antwerp to Zanzibar. More characterful than any global mega-brand, these local goods don't kowtow to foreign marketing concerns. Instead, they bring intrigue to supermarkets worldwide, a trace of the world before marketing grew up.

On my travels, I received stunned looks from a Curacao checkout girl when I offered the lady behind me the entire contents of my new carton of Hardon Tea. In Dubai I was actually arrested, so suspicious was my shelf-scanning and muttering of product names. I caused a comic commotion when trying to explain why I didn't want to scratch my lottery card called Piles. The joys of collecting, I've now concluded, simply don't translate.

Of course, English brands have their misadventures in translation. When Ford launched the Pinto it meant 'small penis' to Brazilians; Vauxhall discovered that Nova means 'doesn't go' for Latinos. Mitsubishi rushed to turn the Pajero ('wanker') into Montero for Spanish markets. While most English-speaking manufacturers can't stand being misunderstood, the brands collected here maintain the courage of their convictions. They proclaim their identity with handsome logos and bold drop shadows, whatever we English-speakers might think.

For twenty years now, I've been addicted to the search, to flattening new finds into my rucksack. Shelf Life hunting is infectious, too, a game for all to play. Acquaintances send postcards from the four corners of the earth, telling me of offerings for the cabinet in my hall. When I discovered that my friends Paul and Paula had amassed quite different brands on their travels, this book was born.

We decided that Shelf Life deserves to be celebrated. It makes the world more exciting for us all. It's only too easy to see homogeneity – identical trainer displays and fast-food outlets wherever you land – but if you travel searching humble shop shelves for surprises, you'll find that 'abroad' (even in dire petrol stations and dingy bars) is still exotic and full of joy.

Once you've 'read' Shelf Life, please travel with eyes wide open and enjoy the world's gems before it's too late. Members of this collection are going the way of the dinosaurs, endangered by the spread of blander brands. Bra milk has become 'Natur'. Creamy Fingers were whipped off the market soon after they were launched. International companies negotiate harder for shelf space than locals like Ars (rat poison) or Kräpp (toilet paper). Only rugged individuals will survive globalisation and remain on sale.

Many of these products are still on the shelves today. They lurk in Asia, the Americas, even Europe, to be spotted amongst strange fruit, in dusty desert grocers and swanky eastern supermarkets. Think of Bush or Siemens… Once you are attuned, Shelf Life may turn up anywhere you go.

Rosie Walford

◤ Kocky Powdered vitamin drink
Portugal
100 x 80 x 80mm

▼▼ Gits Poppadams
India
100 x 160 x 40mm

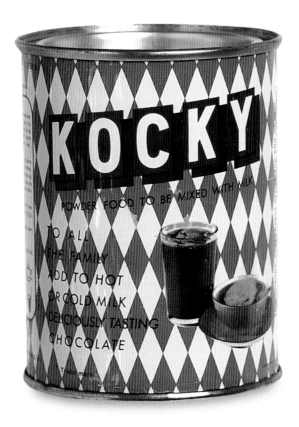

MACHINE MADE

-Gits-
PAPAD

NET
200 g

URAD BLACK PEPPER

COVER
225 PIECES INSIDE

€ 11

▷▷ Looza **Orange juice**
France
173 x 53 x 53mm

▷ Aass Bock Beer
Norway
185 x 60 x 60mm

CONFITE SABOR A CHOCOLAT

CONT. NETO / LÍQUIDO:26 g / NET WT. .9 oz

ERTO CON CARAMELO

dos
en
uno ®

INDUSTRIA CHILENA

▶ Prat **Photo storage**
France
160 x 160 x 1mm

▶▶ De Donkere Sugar
Holland
225 x 95 x 70mm

PRODUITS PHOTOS

PRAT
PRESS BOOK

PHOTO 625

Format utile en cm
Insert size (inch)
Nutzbare Grösse

24x36mm
35mm

▋▋ **B**ienvenue dans le monde professionnel de PRESS BOOK PRAT. Les produits photo : une gamme complète de produits destinés à présenter ou archiver tous les documents photographiques professionnels ou amateurs (films, négatifs, tirages...).

Welcome to the professional world of PRESS BOOK PRAT. Photo products : a complete selection for presentation or archival of all the professional or leisure photographical documents (films, negatives, prints...).

Willkommen in der Welt von PRESS BOOK PRAT. Photo-Produkte : Eine vollständige Produktpalette zur Präsentation und Archivierung aller photografischen Dokumente aus dem professionellen aber auch aus dem Hobby Bereich (z.B Filme, Dokumente, Dias...).

MADE IN FRANCE

PHOTO PRODUCTS

PHOTO PRODUKTE

Packaging design by
Creatio, Paris

$1.6

▶ Lady Gay Hair Wax
Kenya
65 x 90 x 30mm

▶▶ Fogg's Ground coffee
New Zealand
157 x 80 x 40mm

FRESH
- Est. -
FAGG'S ®
- 1926 -
COFFEE

AFTER
DINNER

MULTI-PURPOSE GROUND COFFEE
PLUNGER • PERCOLATOR • FILTER

Medium dark roasted.
A rich, full bodied
nutty flavour.

200g NET

▶ Fairy **Washing up liquid**
United Kingdom
185 x 80 x 55mm

▶▶ Sissy **Biscuits**
Chile
190 x 110 x 40mm

▶ Skum Confectionery
Sweden
185 x 155 x 40mm

▶▶ Dumle Confectionery
Finland
185 x 123 x 15mm

22

▶▶ Sico Condoms
Guatemala
112 x 75 x 20mm

▶ Bulli Corn snacks
Italy
190 x 124 x 56mm

HECHO EN ALEMANIA

SICO®

SENSITIVE®

3 Condones
Anatómicos y Lubricados
Probados Electrónicamente

CONTENIDO: 3 CONDONES

$2.6

RNY

Muesli-barres
Cereal bars

SCHWARTAU

◤ Gross' **White vinegar**
South Africa
240 x 80 x 75mm

◤◤ La Vile **Drinking water**
Vietnam
205 x 60 x 60mm

▶ Schmuck Confectionery
Germany
110 x 110 x 28mm

▶▶ ▶ Slag Pjena Powdered cream
Slovenia
168 x 118 x 10mm

▸ Grizly Savoury snacks ▸▸ Grosso Chewing gum
Chile Spain
175 x 110 x 20mm 20 x 28 x 13mm

£ .33

► Chiky Chocolate biscuits
Costa Rica
100 x 40 x 25mm

►► Slag Lager
Holland
190 x 60 x 60mm

► Love Body Soft drink
Japan
120 x 65 x 65mm

► Flirt Cigarettes
Austria
85 x 55 x 23mm

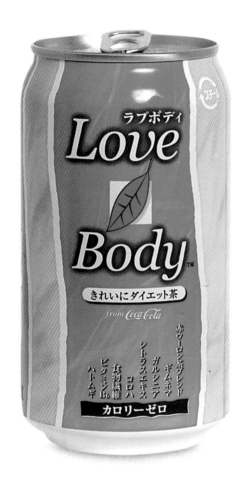

¥ 39

▶▶ Meltykiss Chocolate
Japan
105 x 105 x 55mm

▶ Preen Laundry soap
India
70 x 113 x 30mm

£ · 40

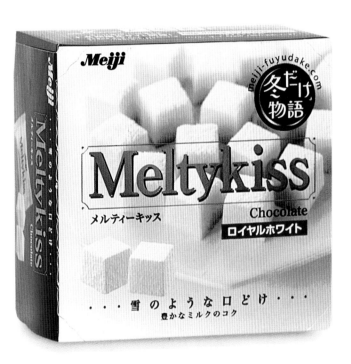

De Beukelaer

Wafeltjes, hazelnootjes, melkchocolade

IRT

Gaufrettes, noisettes, chocolat au lait

▶▶ Frisk Mints
Belgium
33 x 70 x 10mm

▶ Divine Soap
India
58 x 83 x 33mm

50 SUKKERFRI tabletter LAKRISMINT
FR!SK ®
SHARPENS YOU UP!

► Bra **Milk**
Sweden
190 x 70 x 70mm

►► Boo Bee Juice drink
Thailand
133 x 50 x 50mm

BOO BEE

LEMON LIME JUICE

NO PRESERVATIVES

177 ml. NET CONTENT

Products of

▶ Nips Chocolate sweets
Thailand
63 x 122 x 25mm

▶▶ Tit Bits Mouth fresheners
India
110 x 40 x 5mm

▸ Nikka Whisky
Japan
125 x 77 x 63mm

▸▸ Kex Chocolate wafer
Sweden
75 x 230 x 10mm

Fr. .53

▶ Naked **Fruit & nut bar**
New Zealand
48 x 150 x 23mm

date n

ed ™

cashew

40g NET

▼ Horn Chocolate
Japan
100 x 125 x 20mm

▼▼ Dorset Knob Biscuits
United Kingdom
222 x 222 x 100mm

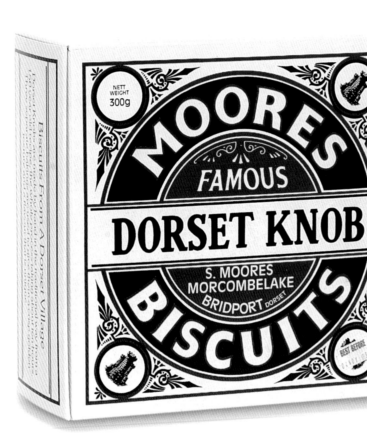

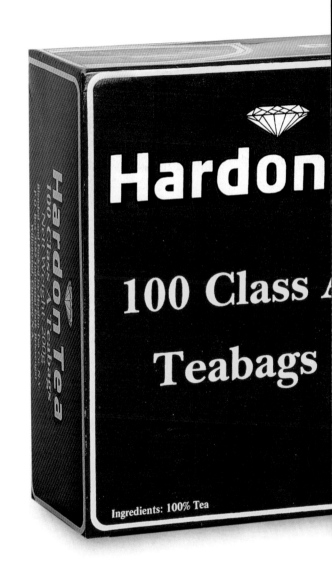

▶ Cock-A-Doodle Soup mix
Jamaica
160 x 130 x 10mm

▶▶ Toss Laundry detergent
Kenya
100 x 85 x 85mm

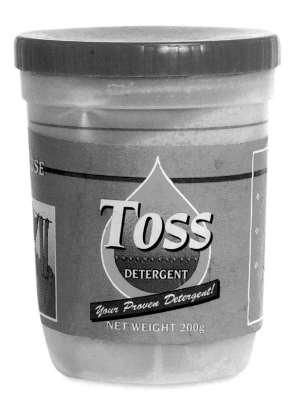

▼ Blow Pop Lollipop
United States
130 x 40 x 30mm

▼▼ Perfect Plus Chocolate
Japan
145 x 33 x 20mm

SWEETENED WITH HONEY

· CAFÉ · FANNY ®

100% ORGANIC

GRANOLA

CAFÉ FANNY

100% ORGANIC

GRANOLA

OUR GRANOLA
is made with oats,
honey, almonds, seeds,
and raisins gathered
from known and
trusted farmers who
are committed to
taking care of the land
for future generations
through organic
and sustainable
agricultural practices.

Delicious with
Fresh Fruit, Yogurt,
Applesauce, Hot
Cereal, Buttermilk,
Ice Cream

You can write to
Café Fanny at
1619 Fifth Street
Berkeley, CA 94710
or telephone us toll-free
at 1-800-441-5413.

NET WT 1 POUND | 16 OZ. | 453 g

▶ Rood Coffee
Holland
130 x 55 x 55mm

▶▶ Lude Boot polish
China
75 x 75 x 20mm

▶▶ Bang Bang Chewing gum
Spain
25 x 95 x 10mm

▶ Chief Whip Cigarettes
United States
73 x 83 x 18mm

Fr. .68

ERB SOAP

PAPORN

39.-

▶ Yes Chocolate
Switzerland
145 x 48 x 30mm

▶▶ Yes Washing up liquid
Sweden
200 x 95 x 55mm

Fr. .74

► Screamers Chewing gum
Ireland
40 x 110 x 30mm

►► Squirt Soft drink
Guatemala
120 x 60 x 60mm

12 OZ FL 355 ml

77

◤ Spunk Confectionery
Germany
54 x 50 x 15mm

▶▼ GSM Wine
Australia
295 x 77 x 77mm

Fr. .78

▶ Cream Fantasy Biscuits
India
240 x 65 x 50mm

▶▶ Golden Stream Drinking water
India
330 x 95 x 95mm

► Fanny Flow CD
Sweden
125 x 125 x 2mm

► Climax **Disinfectant**
►► **Kenya**
65 x 65 x 20mm

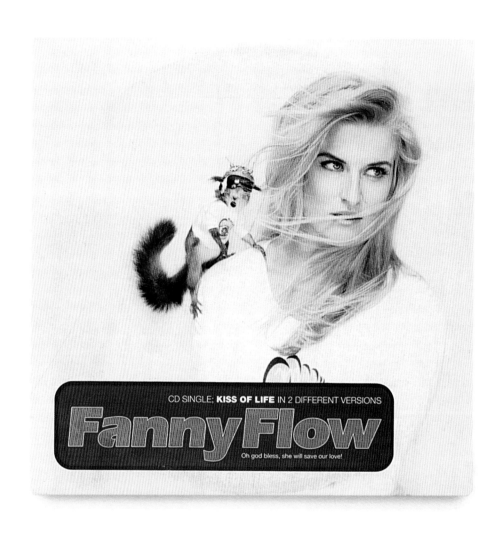

CD SINGLE; **KISS OF LIFE** IN 2 DIFFERENT VERSIONS

FannyFlow

Oh god bless, she will save our love!

▶ Mysore Rose Soap
India
55 x 85 x 25mm

▶▶ SorBits Confectionery
Denmark
43 x 70 x 10mm

85-

▶ Krack Antiseptic cream
India
127 x 30 x 23mm

▶▶ Cocagne **Mackerel fillets**
Portugal
105 x 60 x 28mm

► E Laundry detergent
Poland
208 x 108 x 48mm

►► Tab **Soft drink**
Spain
115 x 70 x 70mm

SIN CAFEINA

TAB

MARCA REG.

GARANTIA DE CO

The Coca-Co

¥91

▶ Amul Butter
India
65 x 18 x 10mm

▶▶ Speed Matches
United Kingdom
50 x 30 x 5mm

▶ E Vitamin supplement
Japan
150 x 85 x 10mm

▶▶ Mental Mints
Italy
50 x 65 x 15mm

▶ Hit Biscuits
Germany
145 x 70 x 70mm

▶▶ Fix Sauce mix
Poland
159 x 129 x 5mm

91·03

Knorr

FIX
do potraw
chińskich

Propozycja podania

▶ Grany Rush **Muesli bars**
Belgium
123 x 143 x 40mm

▶▶ Hype **Energy drink**
Channel Islands
135 x 50 x 50mm

► Happy Turn Savoury snacks
Japan
122 x 165 x 20mm

▼▼ Bliss Alco-pop
United Kingdom
208 x 60 x 60mm

◀ Dazzling Laundry whitener
India
85 x 65 x 33mm

▼▼ Happy Chocolate
Sweden
40 x 145 x 20mm

Fr. 1.03

▶ Grin Toothpaste
Turkey
125 x 20 x 35mm

▶▶ Sparkles Confectionery
New Zealand
20 x 107.5 x 20mm

£ 1·04

► Colon Laundry detergent
Czech Republic
200 x 145 x 53mm

►► Herzgut Butter
Germany
54 x 100 x 28mm

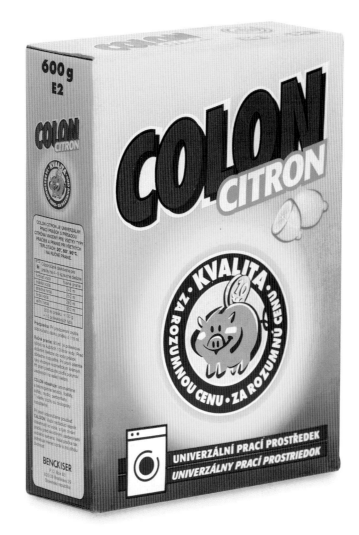

▶ Bum Bums Chewing gum
Spain
30 x 55 x 5mm

▶▶ Pile Scratch card
France
63 x 58 x 1mm

¥ 111

MJUK
LAKRITS-
KOLA

PRIS
GRUPP
8|

▶ WC Kukka **Toilet freshner**
Finland
150 x 98 x 33mm

▶▶ **Guf Confectionery**
Sweden
185 x 140 x 30mm

Fr. 1.17

► Smellur Biscuits
Iceland
65 x 160 x 65mm

►► Rasch Dishwasher powder
Chile
180 x 140 x 38mm

£ 1·18

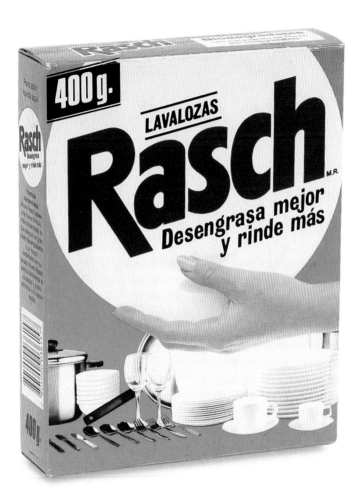

▶ Kalas Dessert mix
Sweden
193 x 130 x 10mm

▶▶ Muecas Childrens' clothes shop
Spain
340 x 220 x 100mm

£1·20

Muecas
Ropa Infantil

C/ Plaza Cardenal Sanz y Fores N° 5
(Plaza Eliptica)
☎ 96 286 70 01
46700 · GANDIA

▶ Pocari Sweat Energy drink
Japan
133 x 51 x 51mm

▶▶ Puke Playing cards
Turkey
90 x 60 x 20mm

► Atum Bom Tuna
Portugal
62 x 105 x 26mm

►► Nuk Rubber teat
Spain
145 x 82 x 35mm

PRODUTO
GARANTIDO

Levante a argola e puxe

ATUM POSTA
EM OLEO VEGETAL

ATUM
BOM
PETISCO

£1·26

NUK®

Tetina antihipo látex
0-6 meses
Tetina ventilada látex
0-6 meses

1

V0.701.128   Rev. 021

La forma NUK diseñada por Dr. med dent A. Müller
y Prof. Dr. W. Balters. / Forma NUK desenhada por
Dr. med. dent. A. Müller e Prof. Dr. W. Balters.

**AIR
SYSTEM**

▶ Wars Sugar
Poland
35 x 45 x 5mm

▶▶ Prison **Body Spray**
Uganda
175 x 45 x 45mm

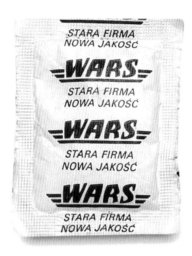

£ 1·28

▶ **Hope Cigarettes**
Japan
70 x 43 x 15mm

▶▶ **Commerce Cigarettes**
Sweden
70 x 55 x 20mm

£1·32

▶▶ Boots Cigarettes
United States
83 x 55 x 23mm

▶ VIP Perfume
Uganda
100 x 55 x 205mm

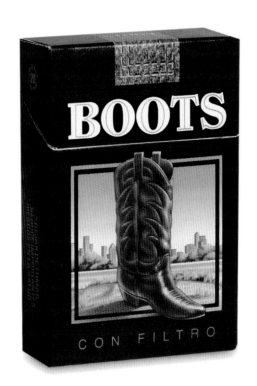

► Invisibles **Pasta**
France
175 x 90 x 70mm

►► **Trick Chocolate wafer**
Jordan
55 x 55 x 15mm

Gefüllte Waffel mit Fruchtzucker-Haselnuß-Nougatcreme für Diabetiker
Zutaten: Zuckeraustauschstoff Fruktose, Haselnußkerne, pflanzl. Öl 1 gehärtet,

frankonia®

Trick®

DIÄT-FRUCHTZUCKER-
NOUGATCREME-WAFFEL

1 BE/KE

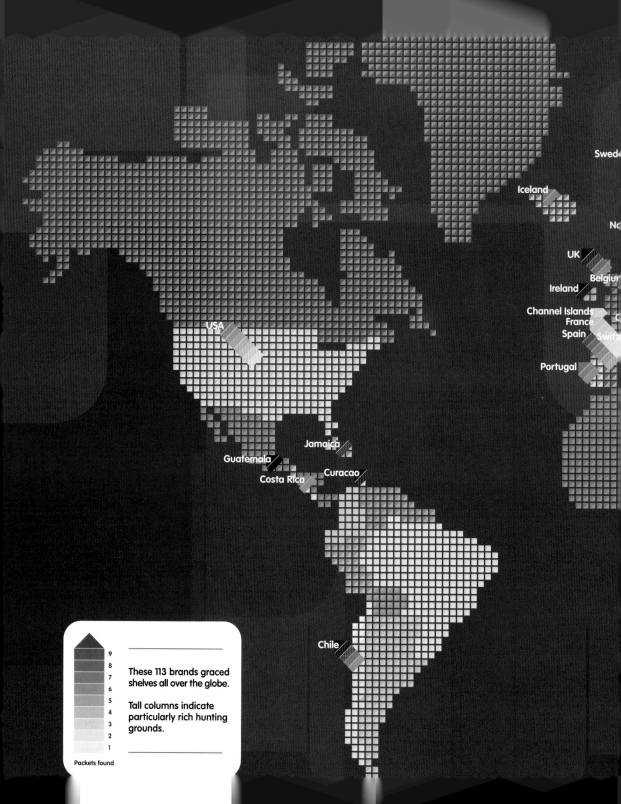

Swede

Iceland

No

UK
Belgium
Ireland
Channel Islands
France
Spain   Switz
Portugal

USA

Jamaica
Guatemala
Costa Rica   Curacao

Chile

9
8
7
6
5
4
3
2
1

These 113 brands graced
shelves all over the globe.

Tall columns indicate
particularly rich hunting
grounds.

Packets found

From Shop Shelf
to Bookshelf

In contrast to the joys of collecting packets, the legalities of this book were no joke. We needed to contact the brands' owners all over the globe. We tried to ask all to sanction our plans.

It turned into a mammoth task. Imagine trying to contact the maker of matches bought eighteen years ago in Tibet. We hired translators in many tongues. Four researchers hammered the phones in patient English. Some we couldn't trace.

While we never meant to ridicule these brands' owners, many were wary of derision. In Peru, the brand manager of the wonderful Grated Fanny was at pains to explain 'we are not interested in your publication. Thanks, but our trade mark "FANNY" was in honour to the owner's sister name (Fanny) and he suppose that your book is a collection of differents and curious trade marks that in english have funny tenses.' [sic]

The German owner of Super Dickmann and Mini Dickmann declined without even a nod to the humour in their name – giving as their reason that 'our products are not currently available in the United Kingdom'. These brands evoke national character to the end.

Yet, despite the clearance struggle, as the publication deadline neared, we continued to text each other from our travels to relay new finds: 'Got Tramp tuna! Tender Nuts! Prick cola!' and debating whether it was too late to squeeze another few into the clearance process. Hundreds of fine packets have not made it into the book – but they're in our ongoing collection, and the search lives on.

★ Marquesa:

Marquesa provide Trade Mark databases and the means to search and report on them. Mercifully, Marquesa's system brings together seemingly incompatible databases from diverse geographical locations and presents them in a thoroughly standardized form.

Marquesa Search Systems Ltd.,
Tel: +44 (0)1647 434100
Email: admin@marquesa.co.uk
Web: http://www.marquesa.co.uk

★ Watson Farley Williams:

Watson Farley Williams are solicitors whose clients include publishers, ad agencies, photographers, designers and producers. They are brilliant at giving practical advice on legal issues affecting the creative industries.

Tel: +44 (0)207 814 8000
Email: nfenner@wfw.com
Web: http://www.wfw.com

★ Ingredients of the Shelf Life collection found by:

Rosie Walford, Paula Benson, Paul West, Colin Greenwood, Julian Walford, Catherine Williamson, Jeremy Panufnik, Anna Pank, John Walford, Tim Nuttall, Veronica Walford, Sarah Newman, Antonella Mancini, Mike Chick, Lucas Hollweg, Rebecca Hollweg, James Bedding, Cathi Du Toit, Jennie Maizels, Manon Van Vark, Tania Unsworth, Tim Webber, Jonathan Cooper, Lydia West, Andy Rumball, Roxanna Macklow-Smith, Sarah King, Roz Davies, Alex Maclean.

★ With added flavouring from:

Charles Walford, Doug Nethery, Nicholas Fenner, Jo Frank, Gavin Hyde-Burke at Carratu, David Sheppard at Compu-Mark.

° Clearance management: Meaghan Kombol ×
×× Database: Christopher Durant #
_ Researchers: Dorothy Atcheson
Shinobu Yamanaka
Olivia Sibony
Sam Knowles __
^ Assistant researchers: Camilla Panufnik
Sebastian Lewis
Lydia West +
Anna Odell +

1 985126 12965

Net 144pp

Index

Aass Bock p12

Amul p92

Atum Bom p126

Bang Bang p69

Basterd, De Donkere p17

Bliss p101

Blow Pop p62

Boo Bee p49

Boots p135

Bra p48

Bulli p24

Bum Bums p110

Chief Whip p68

Chiky p34

Chubi p14-15

Climax p83

Cocagne p89

Cock p60

Colon p108

Commerce p133

Corny p26-27

Cream Fantasy p80

Dazzling p102

Divine p44

Dorset Knob p57

Dumle p23

E p90

E p94

Fagg's p19

Fairy p20

Fanny, Café p65

Fanny Flow p82

Fix p97

Flirt p39

Flirt p42-43

Form p144

Frigor p64

Frisk p45

Gits p11

Golden Stream p81

Grin p104

Grizly p32

Gross' p28

Grosso p33

GSM p79

Guf p115

Happy p103

Happy Turn p100

Hardon p58-59

Herzgut p109

Hit p96

Hope p132

Horn p56

Hype p99

Invisibles p136

Käck p112-113

Kalas p120

Kex p53

Kocky p10

Krack p88

Lay's
p73

 Lady Gay
p18

 Looza
p13

 Love Body
p38

 Lude
p67

 Meltykiss
p41

 Mental
p95

 Mounds
p46-47

 Muecas
p121

 Mysore Rose
p84

 Naked
p54-55

 Nikka
p52

 Nips
p50

 Noisy
p72

 Nuk
p127

Perfect Plus
p63

Personality Puffs
p131

Pile
p111

Plopp
p116-117

Prat
p16

Preen
p40

Prison
p129

 Puke
p123

 Rasch
p119

 Rood
p66

 Rosy
p144

 Rush, Grany
p98

 Schmuck
p30

 Screamers
p76

 Sico
p25

 Sissy
p21

 Skum
p22

 Slag
p35

 Slag Pjena
p31

 Smellur
p118

SorBits
p85

 Sparkles
p105

Speed
p93

 Spunk
p78

 Squirt
p77

Sugar Daddy
p130

Supaporn
p70-71

Sweat
p122

Tab
p91

Tit Bits
p51

 Toss
p61

 Trick
p137

 Vile, La
p29

VIP
p134

 Wars
p128

 WC Kukka
p114

 Yes
p74

Yes
p75

About the Collectors

▼ Rosie Walford

Once a director of international advertising agencies, Rosie spent many years developing branding for global behemoths like Unilever and Mercedes, as well as quirky companies closer to home. Then her love of the wider world took control; she started to roam as a photojournalist, producing travel features and biodiversity picture-stories for the UK's newspapers and weekend magazines.

Nowadays she encourages sustainable creative thinking in companies and campaigning organisations worldwide.

At the same time, she runs a holiday company called The Big Stretch, which takes people walking in wild mountain-scapes to think creatively about their lives. She will always scour shop shelves wherever she goes.

www.thebigstretch.com

▼▼ Paul West and Paula Benson

Paul and Paula are the founders of Form®, an award winning London graphic design consultancy.

Their background lies predominantly in the music industry designing for artists as diverse as Everything But The Girl, Scritti Politti, Busted, Depeche Mode and Natalie Imbruglia. They also enjoy the challenge of corporate identities, books, brochures, websites and moving images.

For further self-expression, Paul and Paula created UniForm®, a rapidly expanding line of urbanwear, vibrant with imagery drawn from contemporary cultural themes including music and snowboarding, which the pair know well.

www.form.uk.com
www.uniform.uk.com